Table of Contents

ASTRO BOY®

14

by
Osamu Tezuka

translation
Frederik L. Schodt

lettering and retouch
Sno Cone Studios

Dark Horse Comics®

publisher
MIKE RICHARDSON

editor
CHRIS WARNER

consulting editor
TOREN SMITH for STUDIO PROTEUS

collection designers
DAVID NESTELLE and LANI SCHREIBSTEIN

English-language version produced by **DARK HORSE COMICS** and **STUDIO PROTEUS**

ASTRO BOY® VOLUME 14

TETSUWAN ATOM by Osamu Tezuka © 2003 by Tezuka Productions. All rights reserved.
English translation rights arranged with Tezuka Productions. ASTRO BOY is a registered
trademark of Tezuka Productions Co., Ltd., Tokyo, Japan. Unedited translation © 2003
by Frederik L. Schodt. All other material © 2003 by Dark Horse Comics, Inc. All rights
reserved. No portion of this publication may be reproduced, in any form or by any means,
without the express written permission of the copyright holders. Names, characters,
places, and incidents featured in this publication either are the product of the author's
imagination or are used fictitiously. Any resemblance to actual persons (living or dead),
events, institutions, or locales, without satiric intent, is coincidental. Dark Horse Comics®
is a trademark of Dark Horse Comics, Inc., registered in various categories and countries.
All rights reserved.

The artwork of this volume has been produced as a mirror-image of the
original Japanese edition to conform to English-language standards.

Published by
Dark Horse Comics, Inc.
10956 SE Main Street
Milwaukie, OR 97222

WWW.DARKHORSE.COM

To find a comics shop in your area, call the Comic Shop Locator Service toll-free
at 1-888-266-4226.

First edition: April 2003
ISBN: 1-56971-895-4

10 9 8 7 6 5 4 3 2 1
Printed in Canada

A NOTE TO READERS

 Many non-Japanese, including people from Africa and Southeast Asia, appear in Osamu Tezuka's works. Sometimes these people are depicted very differently from the way they actually are today, in a manner that exaggerates a time long past or shows them to be from extremely undeveloped lands. Some feel that such images contribute to racial discrimination, especially against people of African descent. This was never Osamu Tezuka's intent, but we believe that as long as there are people who feel insulted or demeaned by these depictions, we must not ignore their feelings.

We are against discrimination, in all its forms, and intend to continue to work for its elimination. Nonetheless, we do not believe it would be proper to revise these works. Tezuka is no longer with us, and we cannot erase what he has done, and to alter his work would only violate his rights as a creator. More importantly, stopping publication or changing the content of his work would do little to solve the problems of discrimination that exist in the world.

We are presenting Osamu Tezuka's work as it was originally created, without changes. We do this because we believe it is also important to promote the underlying themes in his work, such as love for mankind and the sanctity of life. We hope that when you, the reader, encounter this work, you will keep in mind the differences in attitudes, then and now, toward discrimination, and that this will contribute to an even greater awareness of such problems.

— **Tezuka Productions and Dark Horse Comics**

THE WHITE-HOT BEING

First serialized from January to March 1961 in *Shonen* magazine.

8

HI, PROFES-SOR...

ASTRO! COBALT! GREAT TO SEE YOU BOTH!

HMM...

WE PASSED SOME STRANGE GUY IN THE HALL, PROFESSOR... WHO IS HE?

THAT'S *MR. GASTON*, ASTRO... HE'S THE MAN WHO ORDERED THE ROBOT, *BRON-X*...

SO IS BRON-X FINISHED? CAN I SEE HIM?

HA HA HA... I CAN TELL YOU'RE WORRIED... WE'RE STILL IN THE FINAL STAGES OF THE PROJECT...

I SENSE HE'S A *BAD PERSON*, PROFESSOR...

HA HA HA... DON'T WORRY, ASTRO...

YOU CAN TAKE A LOOK AT HIM INSIDE THERE, BUT BE CAREFUL... IT'S TOO DANGEROUS FOR ME TO GET NEAR HIM...

VOOOM

WOW... WHAT A BLAST OF HEAT!

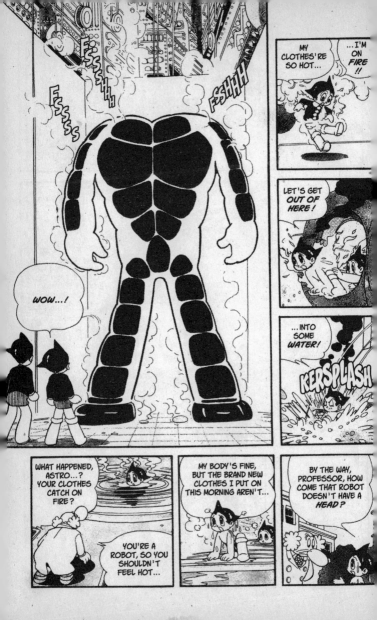

MY CLOTHES'RE SO HOT...

...I'M ON *FIRE!!*

LET'S GET *OUT OF HERE!*

FSSSSS

FSHHH

WOW...!

...INTO SOME *WATER!*

KERSPLASH

WHAT HAPPENED, ASTRO...? YOUR CLOTHES CATCH ON FIRE?

YOU'RE A ROBOT, SO YOU SHOULDN'T FEEL HOT...

MY BODY'S FINE, BUT THE BRAND NEW CLOTHES I PUT ON THIS MORNING AREN'T...

BY THE WAY, PROFESSOR, HOW COME THAT ROBOT DOESN'T HAVE A *HEAD?*

11

12

14

15

16

18

19

20

21

23

THERE'S APPARENTLY NO TRACE OF ASTRO YET...

I'VE HAD ENOUGH!

IF THE POLICE CAN'T FIND HIM...

...I'LL HAVE TO TAKE MATTERS INTO MY *OWN* HANDS!

WHA--?

I'LL HAVE THE BRON-X *BODY* SEARCH FOR ITS OWN HEAD!

B-BUT THAT'S TOO DANGEROUS!!

DANGEROUS?! WHY? A ROBOT WITHOUT A HEAD'S JUST A MECHANICAL DOLL...

AND BESIDES, HIS BODY'S DESIGNED TO KNOW WHERE THE HEAD IS, USING RADIO WAVES... HE'LL FIND IT RIGHT AWAY...

AND MOREOVER, BRON-X'S *STRONGER* THAN ASTRO!!

THERE IS A TINY ISLAND, KNOWN AS *HORAGASHIMA*, IN THE FAR SOUTHERN REACHES OF JAPAN. EVEN THOUGH IT IS SO ISOLATED THAT BIRDS RARELY VISIT, IT NONETHELESS HAS HUMAN INHABITANTS...

ROAR
ROAR

IF I BURY BRON-X'S HEAD HERE, NO ONE'LL *EVER* FIND IT...

SHOOSH
SPLASH

HMPH...

I GUESS I REALLY AM A BAD ROBOT NOW.... I'VE STOLEN SOMETHING, AND BURIED IT, TOO...

I BET THEY'RE REALLY UPSET BACK IN TOKYO...

...BUT I DID THIS FOR THE SAKE OF *HUMANS*...

31

33

34

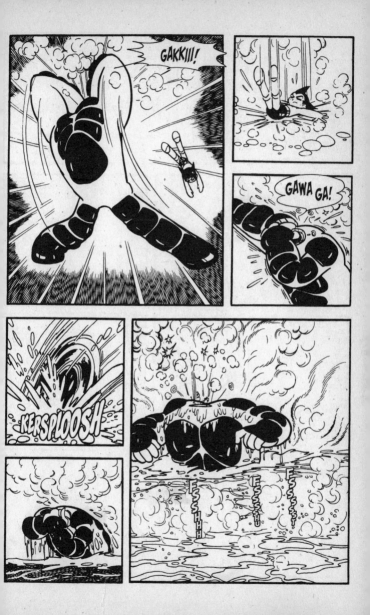

35

37

38

39

40

42

43

44

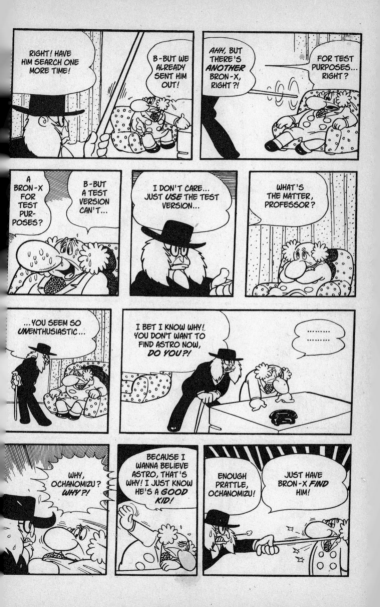

45

46

THERE BRON-X GOES!

THAT SCOUNDREL WASN'T KIDDING!

WELL? ARE YOU CONVINCED?

YES... B-BUT WHO THE HECK *ARE* YOU?!

ME? *AH*, I AM LANKY NOPPO, OF THE C.P. CLUB....

LANKY NOPPO?!

YES... AND PLEASE EXCUSE ME...

NO NEED TO BE SO SURPRISED, MR. GASTON!

JUST IGNORE ME...

HAALP! HE'S A *MONSTER!*

47

48

50

52

53

54

55

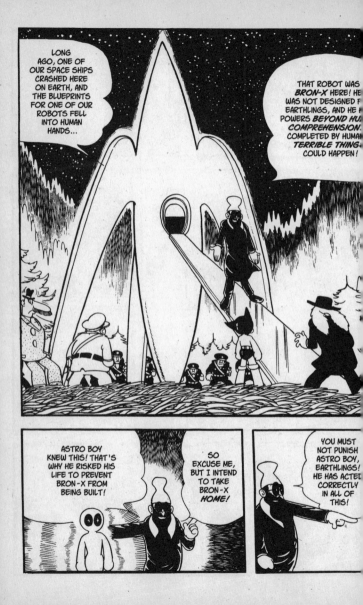

59

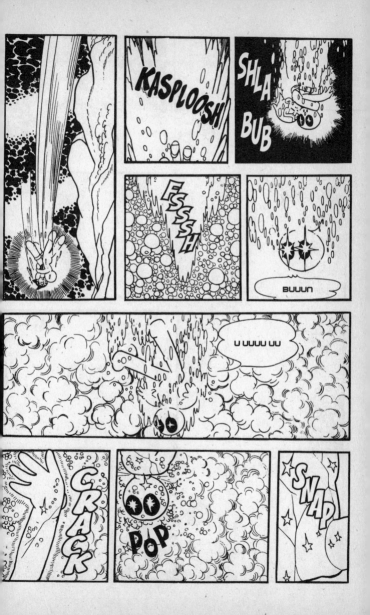

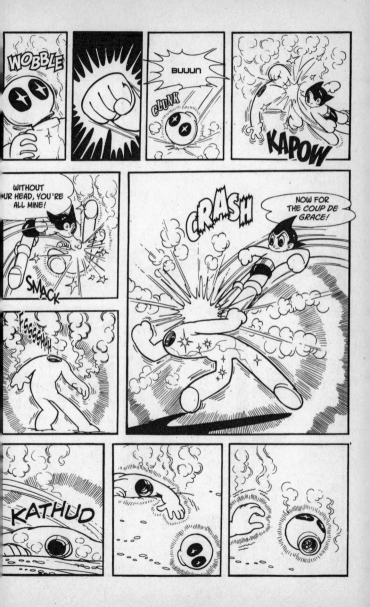

66

URAN

First serialized from August to September
1960 in *Shonen* magazine.

70

71

75

78

79

80

81

83

84

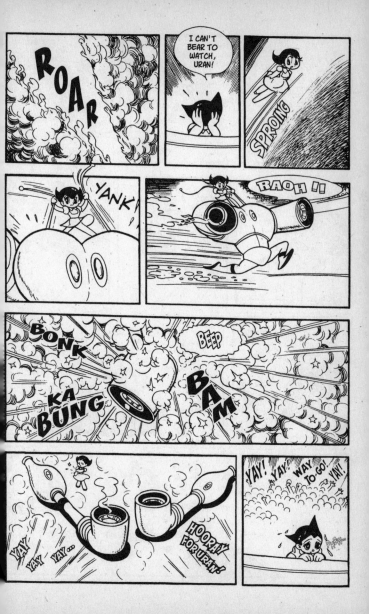

88

89

90

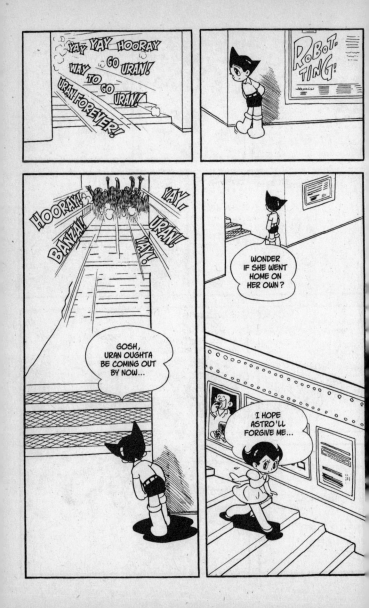

92

93

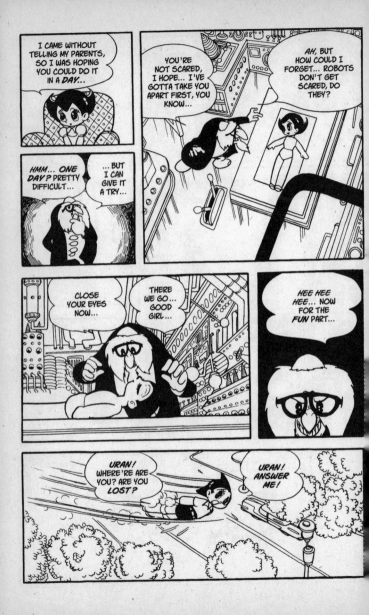

94

96

97

98

100

GOSH, URAN... YOU SURE MADE YOUR OLDER BROTHER *WORRY* A LOT!

≥PHWEW!≤

GUESS I NEVER REALLY HAD ANYTHING TO WORRY ABOUT *AFTER ALL*...

C'N I TALK TO YOU FOR A MINUTE, ASTRO?

URAN WAS ACTING KINDA WEIRD TONIGHT...

AW, C'MON, COBALT... I'VE HAD *ENOUGH* WORRYING ABOUT HER...

Y'KNOW HOW SHE ALWAYS USED TO BRAG ABOUT THE ROBOTTING MATCHES?

WELL, TODAY WAS COMPLETELY DIFFERENT...

SHE DOESN'T REMEMBER ANYTHING 'BOUT THEM AT ALL...

'N SOMETIMES SHE MUMBLES TO HERSELF ABOUT "ONE HALF" SOMETHING OR OTHER...

SHE *WHAT?!*

NOW, KIDS! IF YOU STAY UP TOO LATE, YOU'LL OVERSLEEP TOMORROW!!

DON'T WORRY, DAD... WE'RE GOING TO BED NOW...

G'NITE, DAD!

DO ME A FAVOR, COBALT, AND KEEP AN EYE ON URAN TONIGHT. LET ME KNOW IF YOU SEE ANYTHING WEIRD, OKAY?

GOTCHA...

102

105

107

109

112

116

First serialized from March to June 1963 in *Shonen* magazine.

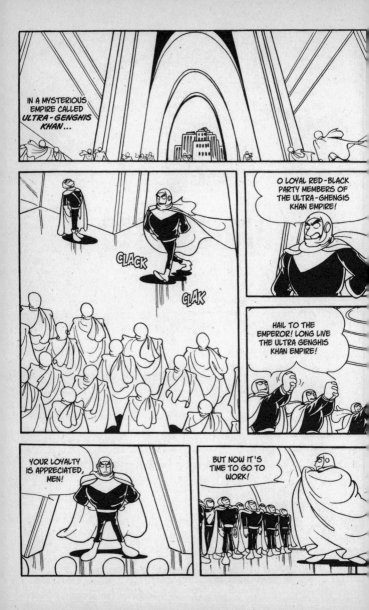

118

119

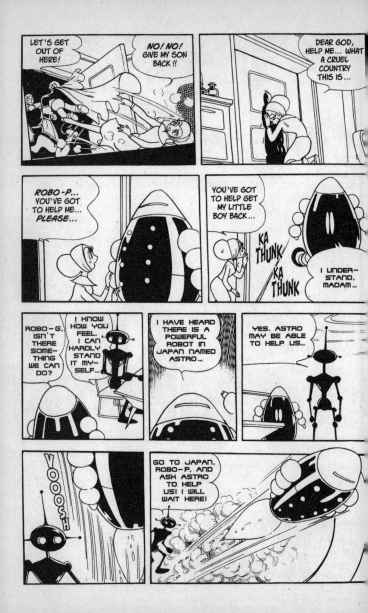

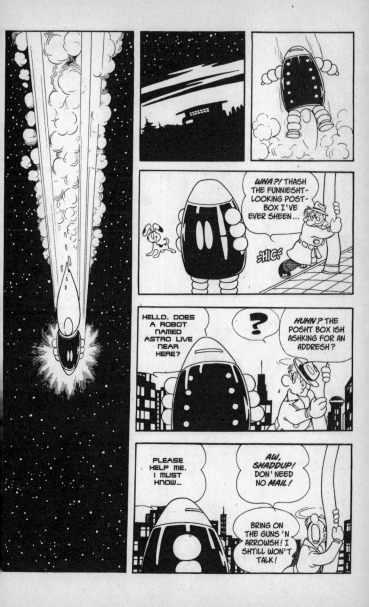

123

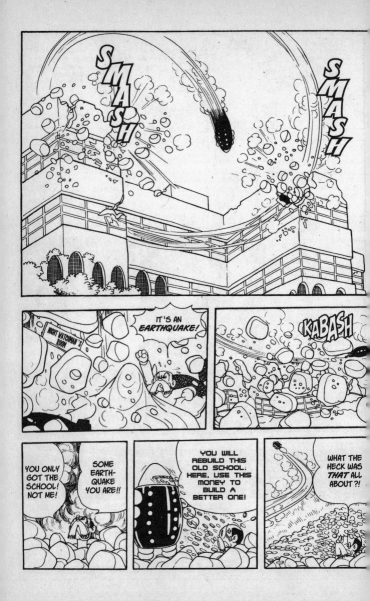

124

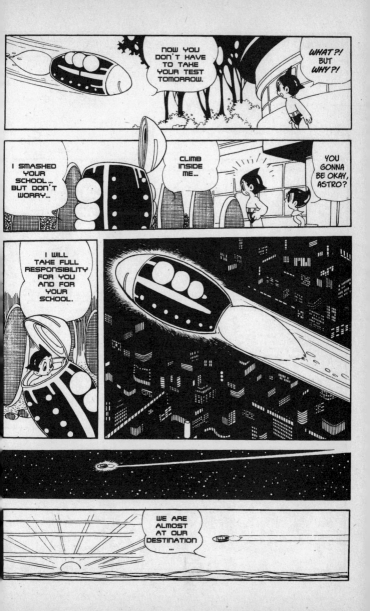

125

130

131

ENOUGH GRUMBLING! TIME FOR YOU GUYS TO GO OUTSIDE!

HEY, LOOKEE!! THEY'RE HOLDING HANDS!!

SHADDUP, KID!!

IT IS NOT GOOD TO ANGER THE RED-BLACK PARTY, ASTRO BOY...

BUT IF I HADN'T DONE THAT, YOU WOULD'VE BEEN *SMASHED!*

IT'S IMPORTANT TO TEACH PEOPLE LIKE THAT A *LESSON!* WHA?!

HUMMMMM

I HEAR A *BOMB!*

KABOOOOM

132

WOW, THAT WAS CLOSE! MUST BE THE *RED-BLACK PARTY* TRYING TO GET *REVENGE!*

I CAN'T BELIEVE HOW *HORRIBLE* THIS GOVERNMENT IS! WHY DOESN'T ANYONE *PROTEST?*

SOMEONE OUGHTA JUST *TOPPLE* THE BAD GUYS!

BUT YOU DON'T KNOW THE *TERRIBLE POWER* OF THE DAMA PALACE, ASTRO!

KA-SHUNK

KA-SHUNK

LOOK! A DAMA PALACE *GUARD* IS LOOKING FOR US!

≥SHH≤... BE *QUIET!*

133

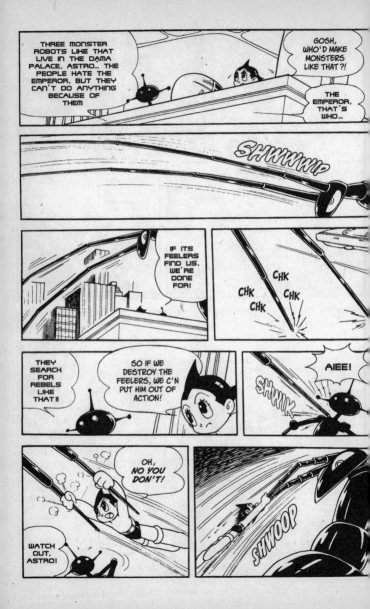

134

135

136

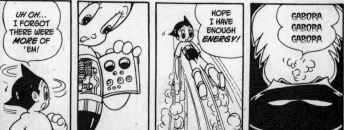

137

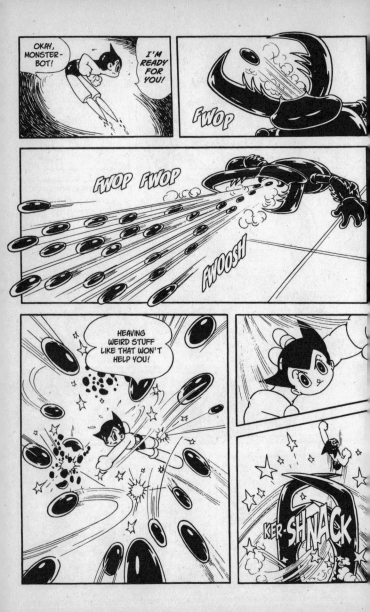

138

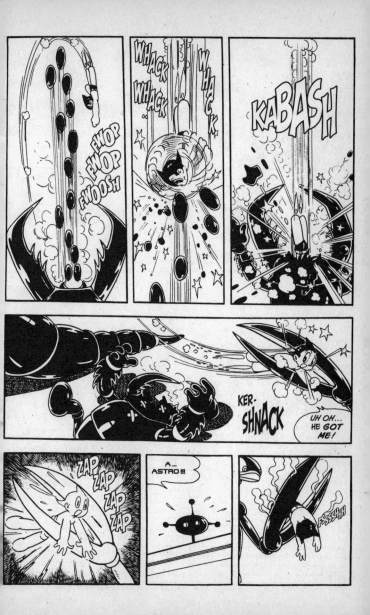

140

144

145

147

148

149

150

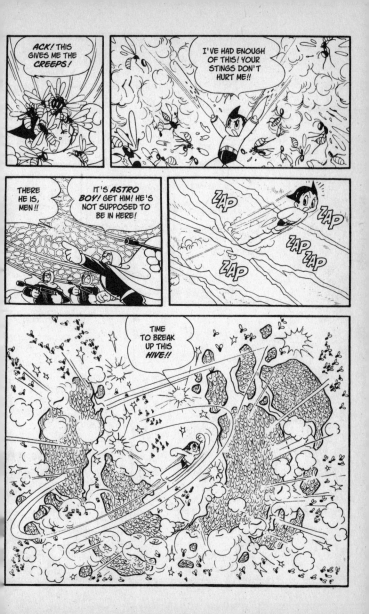

151

152

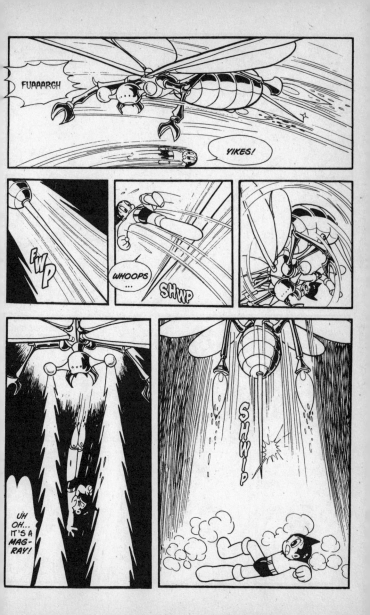

154

156

157

158

159

FORTRESS OF THE CENTAURS

First serialized from May to July 1958 in
Shonen magazine.

166

167

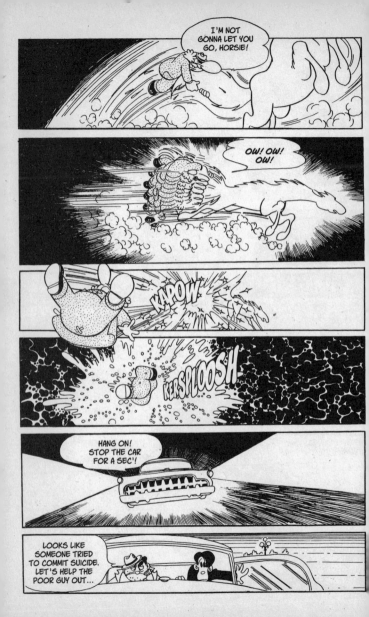

168

169

171

174

177

178

179

182

183

185

186

187

"STILL, SOME OF US WHO COULDN'T FORGET THE HUMAN CHILDREN WHO WERE OUR FRIENDS, DECIDED TO RETURN TO EARTH AFTER ALL..."

"JUST IN CASE, WE TOOK WITH US SPECIAL *GAS PISTOLS*, WHICH COULD BE USED ON HUMANS!"

"IF ANYONE SPOTTED US, THE GAS MADE SURE THEY FORGOT HAVING EVER SEEN US --THE HEAVEN-HORSES, THE *TENMA TRIBE!*"

"UP UNTIL NOW, THOSE OF US WHO RETURNED TO EARTH HAVE BEEN HIDING DEEP IN A *MOUNTAIN FORTRESS.* ONLY OCCASIONALLY DO WE COME DOWN TO WHERE PEOPLE LIVE..."

"THEN WE PLAY WITH A FEW CHILDREN AND HELP THEM GROW TO BE STRONG AND TO BE CLEVER..."

"I, TOO, ONCE DESCENDED TO A VALLEY AND SPOTTED A WONDERFUL BOY WORKING ON A RANCH..."

"I DISGUISED MYSELF AS AN ORDINARY HORSE..."

"I WENT UP TO HIM, AND WE QUICKLY BECAME FRIENDS..."

"THE BOY WAS *KURI-TARO*, OR 'ACORN'..."

"WE RAN AROUND THE HILLS AND FIELDS AND PLAYED TO OUR HEARTS CONTENT."

189

190

191

193

194

196

197

198

200

I STAKED THE FATE OF THE *RED STAR WEEKLY* ON CAPTURING THIS HORSE!!

SORRY, SIR, BUT WE DON'T REMEMBER A THING. WHAT HORSE ARE YOU TALKING ABOUT?

WHEN WE CAME TO, WE WERE TAKING A NAP IN FRONT OF ASTRO BOY'S HOUSE.

THIS HAPPENS TO EVERYONE WHO MEETS THAT HORSE!

THEY *ALL* FORGET WHAT HAPPENED!!

BUT *I* WANNA *KNOW* WHAT HAPPENED... WHAT'D THE HORSE *DO* TO YOU!?

THIS MIKAZUKI? IT'S ME, AKABOSHI... WHAT? *HMM*...

HOKKAIDO? YOU SURE? WHO TOLD YOU?

SO THE BLASTED HORSE ESCAPED TO HOKKAIDO!

MY INSIDE SOURCE TELLS ME HE RAN OFF SOMEWHERE NEAR MT. TOKACHI... *HEH HEH*... GOOD FOOTWORK, NO?

YEAH, HOW'D YOU FIND OUT?

I DON'T CARE WHETHER HE WENT TO MT. TOKACHI OR HABOMAI... I'LL TRACK HIM DOWN!

EASY! WE JUST TURNED THE SCREWS ON *OSAMU TEZUKA*...

LISTEN, MIKAZUKI! I'VE *GOT* TO GO THERE...

I'VE *GOT* TO CATCH THAT HORSE, OR I'LL LOSE FACE!

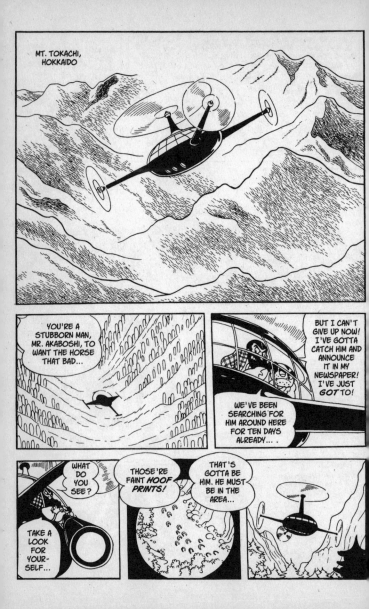

MT. TOKACHI, HOKKAIDO

YOU'RE A STUBBORN MAN, MR. AKABOSHI, TO WANT THE HORSE THAT BAD...

BUT I CAN'T GIVE UP NOW! I'VE GOTTA CATCH HIM AND ANNOUNCE IT IN MY NEWSPAPER! I'VE JUST *GOT* TO!

WE'VE BEEN SEARCHING FOR HIM AROUND HERE FOR TEN DAYS ALREADY...

WHAT DO YOU SEE?

THOSE'RE FAINT *HOOF PRINTS!*

THAT'S GOTTA BE HIM. HE MUST BE IN THE AREA...

TAKE A LOOK FOR YOURSELF...

204

205

207

208

210

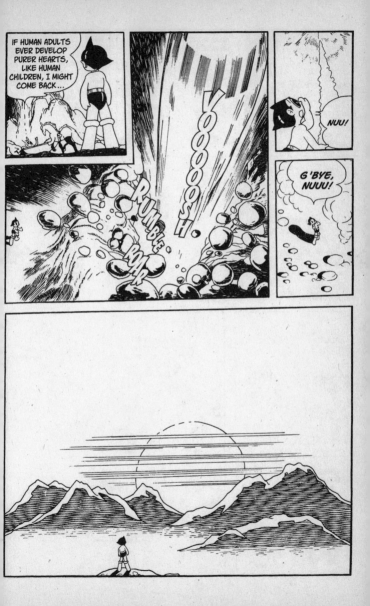

211

GERNICA

First appeared in the special expanded New Year's edition of *Shonen* magazine.

214

KABOOOM BOOM BOOOM BLAM' ROAR SPLOOSH

NOTHING'S WORKING!!

THE MONSTERS'RE APPROACHING *HACHIOJI CITY!* HAJIOJI CITY IS NOW IN DANGER!

LET'S GET OUT OF HERE, ASTRO! EVEN YOU CAN'T TAKE ON THE GERNICA!

HELP THE KIDS EVACUATE, ASTRO! PROTECT 'EM!

NO, TEACHER! I'VE GOTTA *FIGHT* THE GERNICA!

HERE THEY COME !!!

217

219

220

221

ASTRO BOY'S ORIGINS AND HISTORY
PART 2

THE SERIES, *AMBASSADOR ATOM*, IN WHICH ASTRO BOY FIRST APPEARED, STARTED OUT IN A KIND OF CONTRIVED FASHION...

WITH EACH EPISODE I DREW, THE WORK DIDN'T SEEM TO INCREASE MUCH IN POPULARITY...

IN READING RESPONSES FROM READERS ...

...I BEGAN TO WORRY THAT MAYBE I DIDN'T HAVE WHAT IT TAKES TO DO A MAGAZINE SERIALIZATION, THAT MAYBE I WAS REALLY JUST A ONE-SHOT PAPER-BACK ARTIST.

BUT BECAUSE I WAS DOING MORE MAGAZINE SERIALIZ-ATIONS LIKE *ASTRO BOY*, *JUNGLE EMPEROR*, AND *BIBI-CHAN*...

... I DIDN'T HAVE ENOUGH TIME TO SPEND ON THE PAPERBACK BOOKS I WAS DOING, LIKE *FUTURE WORLD*, *CRIME AND PUNISH-IMENT*, AND SO FORTH...

謹賀新年 元旦

"HAPPY NEW YEAR! NEW YEAR'S DAY"

I CREATED THE NEW YEAR'S CARD AT RIGHT IN 1952. IT SHOWS THE CHARACTERS FROM THE FOLLOWING WORKS:
[1+2] *BIBICHAN* ("LITTLE BIBI," THEN SERIALIZED IN *OMOSHIRO BOOK*).
[3+4] *JUNGLE EMPEROR* (KNOWN AS "KIMBA, THE WHITE LION" IN AMERICA, SERIALIZED IN *MANGA SHONEN*)
[5+6] *DEKOBOKO SERIES* ("UNEVEN SERIES"N *MANGA TO YOMIMONO*)
[7] *SABOTEN-KUN* ("CACTUS KID," IN *SHONEN GAHO*)
[8] *BOKU NO SONGOKU* ("MY MONKEY KING," THEN SCHEDULED FOR SERIALIZATION IN *MANGA-O*).
[9] *BOKENKYO JIDAI* ("THE AGE OF ADVENTURES," IN *BOKEN-O*).
[10+11] *AMBASSADOR ATOM*. NOTE THAT THE CHARACTER ATOM (OR ASTRO), DOESN'T APPEAR ANYWHERE. IN OTHER WORDS, IN 1952 ASTRO WAS STILL A BIT-PART PLAYER!

AROUND THAT TIME I MOVED FROM OSAKA TO TOKYO.

...AND ONE DAY I WENT TO VISIT THE EDITORS OF THE MAGAZINE, *SHONEN*.

HI... I'M OSAMU TEZUKA...

GLAD TO MEET YOU. I'M KANAI, THE EDITOR IN CHIEF... THANKS FOR ALL THE SUBMISSIONS YOU'VE MADE...

TO BE PERFECTLY HONEST WITH YOU, TEZUKA...

I THINK YOU WERE RIGHT TO SEND YOUR STORY MANGA TO A *MAGAZINE* FOR SERIALIZATION...

THAT'S GOOD TO HEAR...

THE MAGAZINES TODAY'VE GOT TO GET BEYOND GAG STRIPS....

I THINK THAT WORKS WITH A STRONGER *NARRATIVE* ELEMENT ARE GOING TO BECOME MORE AND MORE POPULAR...

HOW-EVER...

IN THE CASE OF *AMBASSA-DOR ATOM*, WELL, THE STORY SEEMS A LITTLE TOO *SOPHISTI-CATED*...

GOSH... *I* DON'T THINK SO...

THE READERS OF MANGA MAGAZINES AND PAPER-BACK BOOKS ARE QUITE DIFFERENT, YOU KNOW...

IN MANGA MAGAZINES, THE HERO IS THE BIG DRAW...

NOW IN YOUR STORY, THAT ROBOT CHARACTER, ATOM, IS REALLY UNIQUE. WHY NOT MAKE *HIM* THE HERO?

MAKE A *ROBOT* THE HERO? GOSH, THAT SEEMS KIND OF DIFFICULT...

I MEAN, HE'S AN *EMOTION-LESS MACHINE*...

223

"YOUR READERS DON'T REALLY THINK OF ATOM AS A ROBOT, TEZUKA.... THEY THINK HE'S A BOY, LIKE THEM..."

"SO YOU OUGHT TO MAKE HIM MORE LIKE A *HUMAN* CHILD. MAKE HIM A *WARMER*, MORE *EMOTIVE*, HUMAN-LIKE ROBOT... ONE WHO CAN *CRY* AND *LAUGH* AND WHO FIGHTS FOR *JUSTICE*..."

HMM... "A WARMER, MORE EMOTIVE, HUMAN-LIKE ROBOT..."

HOW CAN I MAKE HIM A MORE HUMAN-LIKE ROBOT?

I KNOW... I'LL GIVE HIM A *FAMILY*!

HE'LL NEED *PARENTS*!

SO THAT'S HOW THE FIRST EPISODE OF MIGHTY *ATOM*, OTHERWISE KNOWN AS *ASTRO BOY*, BEGAN... IT WAS THE STORY OF THE CREATION OF ASTRO'S PARENTS -- AND IT'S INCLUDED IN THE FIRST PART OF "GAS PEOPLE" IN VOLUME 15 OF THIS SERIES.

THE END

224